D

EARTH'S
NATURAL
BIOMES

DESERT BIOMES

Louise and Richard Spilsbury

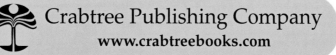
Crabtree Publishing Company
www.crabtreebooks.com

Crabtree Publishing Company
www.crabtreebooks.com
1-800-387-7650

Published in Canada
Crabtree Publishing
616 Welland Avenue
St. Catharines, ON
L2M 5V6

Published in the United States
Crabtree Publishing
PMB 59051
350 Fifth Ave, 59th Floor
New York, NY 10118

Published in 2018 by CRABTREE PUBLISHING COMPANY.

First published in 2017 by Wayland
Copyright © Wayland, 2017

Authors: Louise Spilsbury, Richard Spilsbury

Editors: Hayley Fairhead, Philip Gebhardt

Design: Smart Design Studio

Map (page 7) by Stefan Chabluk

Editorial director: Kathy Middleton

Proofreader: Crystal Sikkens

Prepress technician: Tammy McGarr

Print and production coordinator: Margaret Amy Salter

Photographs

All photographs except where mentioned supplied by Nature Picture Library www.naturepl.com

Front cover(main) and p20(inset) Solvin Zanki; cover (tr), title page(main), p4 and p31(br) Steve O. Taylor (GHF); p5 Ann & Steve Toon; p6 and back cover(r) Rolf Nussbaumer; p7 Chris Mattison; p8, back cover(l) and title page(b) Rolf Nussbaumer; p9(main) Jack Dykinga, p10 and front cover(tl) Bruno D'Amicis; contents page(t) and p11(main) Stefan Widstrand; title page(t), p12(main) and p31(t) Solvin Zankl; imprint page(b) and p13 Ben Cranke; p14 Konstantin Mikhailov; p15 and p31(bl) Daniel Heuclin; p16 Fred Olivier; contents page(b) and p17 Visuals Unlimited; p18 Dave Watts; p19 and p32 Jose B. Ruiz; front cover(b) and p21(main) Marguerite Smits Van Oyen; p21 John Cancalosi; p22 Chadden Hunter; p23 Gavin Hellier; p25 Eric Baccega; imprint page(t) and P26 Daniel Heuclin; p27 Staffan Widstrand; p28 Roladn Seitre; p29 Ann & Steve Toon.

Photographs supplied by Shutterstock: p9(inset) Shihina; p11(inset) Laborant; p12(inset) EcoPrint; p24 Lukas Holub.

Printed in the USA/122019/BG20171102

Library and Archives Canada Cataloguing in Publication

Spilsbury, Louise, author
    Desert biomes / Louise Spilsbury, Richard Spilsbury.

(Earth's natural biomes)
Includes index.
Issued in print and electronic formats.
ISBN 978-0-7787-3992-0 (hardcover).--
ISBN 978-0-7787-4005-6 (softcover).--
ISBN 978-1-4271-2002-1 (HTML)

    1. Desert ecology--Juvenile literature. 2. Deserts--Juvenile literature. I. Spilsbury, Richard, 1963-, author II. Title.

QH541.5.D4S64 2018   j577.54   C2017-906883-0
                          C2017-906884-9

Library of Congress Cataloging-in Publication Data

Names: Spilsbury, Louise, author. | Spilsbury, Richard, 1963- author.
Title: Desert biomes / Louise Spilsbury, Richard Spilsbury.
Description: New York, New York : Crabtree Publishing Company, 2018. | Series: Earth's natural biomes | Includes index. |
Identifiers: LCCN 2017051154 (print) | LCCN 2017054838 (ebook) |
   ISBN 9781427120021 (Electronic HTML) |
   ISBN 9780778739920 (reinforced library binding) |
   ISBN 9780778740056 (pbk.)
Subjects: LCSH: Desert ecology--Juvenile literature. | Deserts--Juvenile literature. | Desert conservation--Juvenile literature.
Classification: LCC QH541.5.D4 (ebook) |
LCC QH541.5.D4 S6495 2018 (print) | DDC 577.54--dc23
LC record available at https://lccn.loc.gov/2017051154

CONTENTS

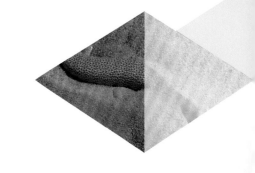

WHAT IS A DESERT BIOME?

Most people think of deserts as hot and sandy, but there are several different kinds of desert. What makes a desert a desert is a lack of rain. Most deserts get less than 10 inches (25 cm) of rain a year, whereas 80 inches (200 cm) can fall in a rainforest every year.

Different deserts

Some deserts are large, flat expanses of sand, but others have rocks and mountains or hills of sand, called dunes, that can reach 1300 feet (400 m) high. Some deserts reach sizzling temperatures of 130°F (54°C) or more, while other deserts have chilly winters or are freezing cold all year, like Antarctica. Some deserts receive very light but regular rain showers, others get all their annual rain in one heavy storm that lasts for just an hour.

Only one in ten of the world's deserts has sand dunes. Most, like this one in northern Niger, are rocky with occasional plants.

Fact Focus: Biome or Habitat?

Biomes are regions of the world, such as deserts, forests, rivers, oceans, tundra, and grassland, that have similar **climate**, plants, and animals.
A habitat is the specific place in a biome where a plant or animal lives.

Desert life

Some deserts look empty and lifeless. The lack of water and soil means that plants grow far apart, to get a share of any water available. But there is a rich variety of plant life, ranging from saguaro cacti as tall as a four-story house to plants that look like tiny stones (see page 9). There are few trees to give shade, so although there are some large animals, such as camels, most desert-dwelling animals are small. Some, such as desert tortoises, have shells or tough, scaly skin to protect them from the fierce temperatures. Others, such as ground squirrels, make burrows under the ground to escape the daytime heat.

The Cape ground squirrel has a long, very bushy tail that it uses like an umbrella to provide shade when it is feeding in the hot Kalahari Desert.

Amazing Adaptation

Adaptations are special features or body parts that living things develop over time to help them survive in a biome. **Mammals**, such as camels, that live in hot deserts have very furry backs to protect them from the burning sun.

WHERE ARE DESERTS?

There are four different types of deserts—subtropical, coastal, semi-arid, and polar—that cover about one fifth of Earth's land surface.

Subtropical deserts

Many of the world's deserts, including the Sahara Desert in Africa and the Sonoran Desert in North America, are subtropical. Very hot, moist air rises above the **equator**, condenses and falls as heavy tropical rains in rain forests. The air is now very dry as it moves to the north and south of the equator, creating deserts in subtropical areas.

Polar deserts

Antarctica is the driest desert of all. More than 98 percent of Antarctica is covered with ice and there is no rain, only snow, so there is almost no liquid water at all.

Amazing Adaptation

The Couch's spadefoot toad sheds layers of skin to create a watertight covering over its body. This prevents water from escaping from the toad's body, helping it survive dry periods underground. These toads can eat enough **insects** in one or two nights to survive for up to a year.

The Sonoran Desert has two short rainy seasons, and then it's dry for months. Couch's spadefoot toads stay underground for most of the year and only come out when it rains.

Coastal deserts

When air blows over a coast from a cold ocean, the **water vapor** in the air condenses to form fog. If the water droplets in this fog are too small to fall as rain, they **evaporate** in the hot daytime sun. This lack of moisture creates coastal deserts, such as the Atacama Desert in Chile and the Namib Desert of South Africa.

Semi-arid deserts

Semi-arid deserts are also known as cold winter deserts. They have dry summers and cold winters with very little rain or snow. Large mountain ranges often block precipitation from falling in these areas. This is known as the rain shadow effect. The Gobi Desert in central Asia and the Great Basin Desert in the USA are semi-arid deserts.

Some deserts are caused by more than one factor. The Atacama is a coastal desert and experiences a rain shadow effect from the Andes Mountains.

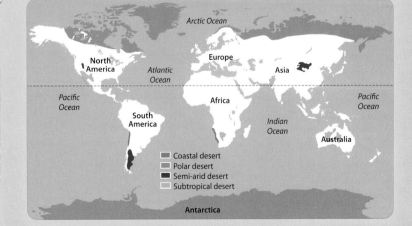

This map shows the location of the four different types of desert found around the world.

DESERT PLANTS

While there are different plants in hot deserts around the world, many have similar adaptations for surviving the heat and lack of water. Some desert plants grow all year, while others seem to magically reappear after heavy rains.

Collecting water

To collect water from droplets of fog or sudden rains, some desert plants, such as yuccas and agaves, have roots that spread far and wide just below the surface. Other plants, such as mesquite, have very long roots that reach water stores called **aquifers** deep underground. Many desert plants are succulents. These plants have thick fleshy stems, often with folds or grooves in them, which can swell to store water for use during the long dry periods.

Desert cacti provide food and shelter for a variety of desert animals. Tiny hummingbirds beat their wings quickly to hover at cactus flowers to sip their **nectar**.

Amazing Adaptation

Cactus plants are perfectly adapted for life in the desert. Cactus stems have folds that expand to store water after it rains. Their leaves are thin spines to minimize water loss.

Desert defenses

Many desert plants have thorns or spikes to deter animals from eating them to get at their water supply. Living stone plants are **succulents**. When their leaves swell with stored water they look like the stones around them. This clever disguise hides the plants from animals that might try to eat them!

Living stone plants look like tiny stones. You can only tell they are plants when they flower!

After heavy rains, some empty-looking deserts, such as this one in Arizona, USA, are suddenly covered with a carpet of brightly colored flowers.

Instant flowers

Some desert plants, such as mallow, sand verbena, and prickly poppies, usually only appear after heavy rains. They grow when the ground is soaked and produce flowers and seeds very quickly. The seeds have a thick outer coat that allows them to survive underground for a long time. When it rains again, they burst into life!

SUBTROPICAL DESERT LIFE

Animals that live in subtropical deserts face many challenges. The only places where temperatures are higher than the daytime temperatures here are inside volcaoes. There are few clouds to stop the heat from escaping, so the nights are very cold.

Furry fox

In the Sahara Desert, the fennec fox digs large burrows to escape the daytime heat. It comes out at night to hunt when it is cooler. Fennec foxes hunt animals, such as insects and **reptiles**. They get all the water they need from their food. Thick fur on the fox's back protects it from the blazing sun and keeps it warm at night. The sandy-colored fur **camouflages** it in the desert and absorbs less heat than dark fur.

The fennec fox is small, but its ears can be half the length of its body!

Amazing Adaptation

The fennec fox's big ears help it hear **prey** moving around in the dark. They also help to keep it cool. As warm blood passes through the many **blood vessels** in their large ears, heat escapes into the air.

Shifting sands

Subtropical deserts are usually sandy or coarse and rocky. Sand is tricky to move across because it can shift and it can also get very hot. Fennec foxes have fur around their paw pads to protect their feet from hot sand and help them grip the sand better. Camels have large, flat feet to spread their weight which stops them from sinking into the sand. Sand fish lizards are named for the way they "swim" just below the surface of the hot sand!

Amazing Adaptation

Camels have long eyelashes to keep wind-blown sand out of their eyes. They can also close their nostrils, so they can walk safely through a sand storm.

Sand fish lizards have a long, narrow body, short legs and a pointed snout to help them move quickly beneath the sand.

COASTAL DESERT LIFE

Coastal deserts have cool winters to provide relief after the long, warm summers. Wildlife can also access year-round moisture from early-morning fog.

Trapping water

In the early morning, the Namib fog-basking beetle climbs to the top of a sand **dune** for a drink. It stands on its front legs with its body raised at an angle above its head. Fog blows in from the sea and water droplets in the fog stick to tiny bumps on its hard wings. Many droplets form drops that roll down waterproof grooves between the bumps and fall straight into the beetle's mouth!

The Namib fog-basking beetle, no bigger than a fingernail, collects its water supply from morning fog.

Amazing Adaptation

The weird Welwitschia plant of the Namib Desert has long, drooping leaves that spread out across the land. Water droplets from morning fog **condense** on the leaves, which channel the droplets into the ground for the roots to soak up.

Desert chameleons

Most chameleons wait for prey to come to them, but those that live in deserts have to work harder because food is scarce. The Namaqua chameleon has toes that spread apart to stop it from sinking in the Namib Desert sand and help it run fast. It uses it long tongue to catch anything it can swallow, such as beetles, snakes, and scorpions. This amazing animal has one other trick up its sleeve. In the morning, when it needs to warm up, it changes to a very dark color to absorb the heat. In the hottest part of the day, it changes to a very light color to keep cool.

The Namaqua chameleon's tongue is twice as long as its body, and has a swollen sticky tip that shoots out to capture prey.

Fact File: Namib Desert

Location: West coast of southern Africa
Size: 31,274 sq. mi. (81,000 km^2)
Overview: The Namib Desert has vast gravel plains, scattered mountains, and sand dunes that rise up to 1000 feet (300 m) tall. Succulents grow near the coast, but elsewhere there are very few plants.

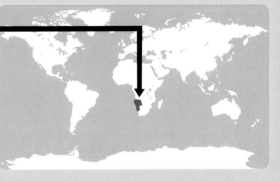

SEMI-ARID DESERT LIFE

Semi-arid deserts can be extreme places for animals to live. The Gobi Desert is very dry and has icy winters and burning hot summers.

Gobi gerbils

One animal that manages to survive in the Gobi Desert is the gerbil. Gerbils have sharp claws for digging underground burrows to escape danger and extreme temperatures. In summer they collect and store food, such as seeds, to survive the winter, when food is scarce. Groups of gerbils can stay underground for months when it is freezing. These tidy animals dig different burrows for storing food, sleeping, and using as a toilet!

The Mongolian gerbil's sand-colored fur helps to camouflage it from **predators**. If a bird or snake grabs the gerbil by the tail, it loses its tail to escape, and grows a new tail later!

Fact File: Gobi Desert

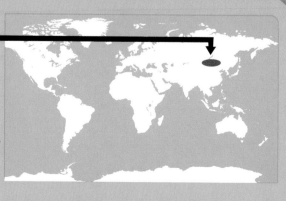

Location: Mongolia and China
Size: 494,000 sq. mi. (1,300,000 km²)
Overview: A sandy and rocky desert surrounded on three sides by mountains. It is so dry that there are few plants.

Rattlesnakes

Great Basin rattlesnakes escape the daytime heat of the Great Basin Desert by hiding in rock caves or underground burrows of other animals. In the winter, they **hibernate** in spaces in rocks to survive the cooler temperatures. Rattlesnakes also hunt for food in burrows. They have heat sensing **pits** behind each nostril that detect the heat given off by animals, such as mice and rats. This helps them to find their prey even in the total darkness underground. They bite into victims with their long fangs. The fangs inject **venom** that stuns prey so the snake can swallow it more easily.

A rattlesnake can shake the rattle at the end of its tail 60 or more times per second. Snakes grow by shedding old skin. Some rings of skin stay on the tail and harden to form rattles.

Amazing Adaptation

A rattlesnake's colors camouflage it in the desert, but if predators, such as eagles spot it, the rattlesnake hisses and rattles its tail to scare them away.

POLAR DESERT LIFE

The central desert region of Antarctica has so little water it is almost plant-free. It is colder here than anywhere else on Earth. Most of its wildlife is found on the coast, where the weather is milder.

Bird life

Some birds called petrels make nests on the bare rock on top of mountains that peek through the ice sheets. Giant petrels feed on penguins and other birds, as well as fish and squid from the ocean. Penguins have a thick layer of fat called **blubber** so they can survive on land and in the icy ocean, where they catch fish. Their short densely packed feathers help to keep out icy winds.

Male emperor penguins huddle together in the Antarctic desert to keep warm while they care for their chicks.

Amazing Adaptation

Most penguins build nests from piles of stones to protect their eggs from the cold. When a female emperor penguin lays an egg she passes it to the male. He balances it on his feet to keep it off the ice and nestles it among his feathers to keep it warm.

Leopard seals

Leopard seals are found around the edges of the Antarctic **continent**. Like Antarctic penguins, leopard seals have a thick layer of blubber to **insulate** them from the cold. Leopard seals feed in the water and use their powerful jaws and long teeth to catch smaller seals, fish, and squid. They haul themselves out onto ice sheets to rest. Females also give birth to their pups on the ice sheets and dig small snow holes to keep their young safe while they grow.

Leopard seals are 10 to 13 feet (3 to 4 m) long and are named because of their spotted fur. They move quickly and catch prey in the water and on the ice using their huge mouth full of sharp teeth.

Fact File: McMurdo Dry Valleys

Location: Antarctica, south of the Ross Sea
Size: 1825 sq. mi. (4800 km²)
Overview: The driest part of a huge, icy continent, found a few miles from the coast. There are giant slow-moving rivers of ice called glaciers. There is no rainfall and very little snowfall throughout the year. The few living things in McMurdo include lichens, mosses, and tiny animals, such as nematode worms.

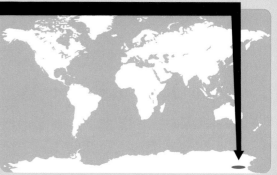

BORN SURVIVORS

Desert animals have some clever ways to make sure their young survive the extreme heat and the threat from predators.

Cactus homes

A spiky cactus might not seem like a very cozy place to bring up babies, but several desert birds build their nests in these plants because the spikes keep eggs and chicks safe from predators. For example, great horned owls build awkward-looking nests from sticks. Cactus wrens make nests from grasses with an opening at one end. Gila woodpeckers lay about four white eggs in a nest inside a saguaro cactus!

Inside the cactus, the gila woodpecker's eggs and chicks are kept cool and safe from predators.

Amazing Adaptation

Gila woodpeckers have very strong head and neck muscles, and a long, hard, pointed beak. They use these body parts to peck holes in saguaro cacti when building their nests.

Spider moms

Most spider mothers leave once they lay their eggs, but the tarantula is worse—she tries to eat her young! After she lays about 1,000 eggs in an underground burrow, the female tarantula seals it with a cover of silk. The eggs hatch after seven weeks and the young spiderlings cut holes in the silk cover and race away before their mother comes back to eat them!

Some desert spiders make excellent mothers, however. Female wolf spiders lay hundreds of eggs and wrap them in a bag of silk. They carry their eggs everywhere they go and search for them if they drop off. When the eggs hatch, the spiderlings climb up their mother's legs onto her back. They are safe from predators here. They stay on her back for several days until they are old enough to feed and defend themselves.

By carrying her eggs and babies, the wolf spider can keep them at a comfortable temperature and protect them from predators.

DESERT FOOD CHAINS

A desert **food chain** tells the story of who eats who in the biome.
Plants, such as cacti, use **energy** from the sun to make food.
Some animals get the energy they need by eating plants.
Others get their energy by eating other animals.

Energy in the Kalahari food chain flows from cacti and other plants, to eagles, via scorpions and meerkats.

Kalahari killers

Insects called termites build tall mounds of mud to get shelter from the Kalahari Desert's heat. They eat plants, such as dead cacti. Scorpions eat termites, and meerkats enjoy a tasty scorpion or two! They quickly and carefully bite off the scorpion's stinger and spit it out so they can eat the animal. Meerkats take turns watching for predators, while others feed. If the "guards" spot an eagle, they call out and all the meerkats run for safety in underground burrows.

Amazing Adaptation

The meerkat's long snout can sniff out scorpions and insects that hide in burrows by day. They use their curved claws to quickly dig holes in the sand to get their prey.

Scorpions get energy by eating prey such as termites. A scorpion catches its prey in its pincers and then injects the prey with deadly venom before eating it.

Cleaning up deserts

In deserts, as in other biomes, there is a lot of natural waste to clear up, including the remains of animals that predators have killed and fed on. Other animals may have simply died of natural causes such as old age. Scavengers are animals, such as vultures, and coyotes, that feast on these sources of dead meat.

The final links in the desert food chain are decomposers such as bacteria fungi, and earthworms. Decomposers eat fallen leaves, dead plants, animal poop and other waste including the remains left over by scavengers. They gain energy as they feed, but in the process also release nutrients into the soil that plants can use to grow and start new desert food chains.

Nothing is wasted in a desert. This turkey vulture scavenges the dried and rotting remains of a wild pig.

Fact Focus: Food Webs

Several food chains together form food webs. For example, desert termites are eaten by many animals from scorpions to toads, lizards, and birds, and lizards may be eaten by many types of birds and snakes.

PEOPLE IN THE DESERT

The deserts of the world may lack water and suffer extreme temperatures, but they are still home to hundreds of millions of people!

Traditional lives

Some people who live in deserts grow crops on land around an **oasis**. An oasis is a place where water rises to the surface from an underground river, spring, or aquifer. An aquifer is a layer of underground rock with holes that hold or allow water to run through. Some farmers are **nomads**. They travel around and live in tents so they can move their flocks of goats, sheep, and camels to places where there are plants for the animals to eat.

Desert people often wear light–colored robes because light colors **reflect** rather than absorb the sun's rays.

Amazing Adaptation

People have adapted to living in deserts by constructing buildings that keep them cool. Some buildings have tall wind towers that capture breezes high above ground level and carry the cooler air deep inside. These towers also allow hot air to escape. Openings and windows are often small and kept in the shade by overhanging roofs.

Growing cities

There are also huge cities that have been built in the middle of deserts, such as Dubai in the Arabian Desert and Las Vegas in the Mojave Desert. To get the water needed for drinking, washing, cooking, and to grow large fields of crops for cities, people pump water up from deep aquifers. In some places they also redirect rivers to water plants. Water from the Colorado River is piped to the desert in Imperial Valley, California, to grow food.

Las Vegas is a huge city in the Mojave Desert, one of America's smallest and driest deserts.

Fact Focus: Water Problems

Desert aquifers are often filled with water from rain that fell a long way away and slowly flowed there underground. When people take too much aquifer water for big farms or cities, plants that rely on this water cannot get enough to grow. Desert animals are then left without any food to eat.

DESERT RESOURCES

Deserts may look empty, but beneath the rock, sand, and gravel there are hidden treasures that people can use.

Finding fuels

Some deserts hold massive amounts of oil and gas below their surface. Oil companies often have to drill down hundreds of feet to reach oil and gas supplies. Then pipelines carry the fuels for hundreds of miles across deserts to ports. From here, giant ships called tankers deliver it to buyers.

This is an oil well in the United Arab Emirates. Millions of years ago, the region was covered in ocean water. Animals that died in these ancient seas gradually formed fossil fuels.

Fact Focus: Antarctic Resources

So far, the Antarctic desert's resources are untapped because no one country owns Antarctica. Nations of the world have signed an Antarctic Treaty that allows them to carry out scientific research there, but not to do any drilling for oil or **minerals**. One reason is that transporting oil from here by ship would be risky and oil spills could ruin this wild habitat.

Mining minerals

There are also useful and valuable minerals, such as gold and copper beneath deserts. Gold is used to make things such as jewelry. Copper is a metal that electricity can flow through so it is used to make things such as electrical wire.

People dig mines to reach desert minerals like these. The problem is that miners may use substances to extract minerals from rocks that can **pollute** desert aquifers. They also use water to clean minerals. This reduces the amount of water available for plants.

Fact Focus: Salt Mines

In some places people dig for salt, too. The salt is found in desert regions where there were seas millions of years ago. As the water evaporated, salt was left behind.

These men are digging up slabs of salt from the desert in Ethiopia.

DESERT THREATS

The desert is an important and useful biome, but parts of it are at risk of being damaged and destroyed forever.

Global warming

Deserts are not only losing water to big cities and farms, they are also becoming drier due to **global warming**. Global warming is the gradual increase in Earth's temperature. Rising temperatures cause droughts. When little or no rain falls, more water evaporates from the soil and causes oases to dry up.

Dorcas gazelles in the Sahara Desert can get all the water they need from plants they eat. However, **drought** and overgrazing reduce the plant life and put these beautiful animals at risk.

Fact Focus: Animals Under Threat

Droughts reduce the plant life that grows in deserts and when it is hotter animals spend more time in burrows. This means there is less food for desert animals to eat and they have less time to find it.

Overgrazing

Overgrazing is when farmers allow too many cattle, goats, or sheep to feed on an area of land where there are few plants. The farm animals eat all the plants, and their hooves damage the newly bare soil, making it even drier and dustier. This makes it harder for new plants to grow there, leaving fewer plants for wild desert animals to eat in the future.

Habitat destruction

People take over desert habitats when they build towns, roads, and mines. Rare animals, such as gray kangaroos, risk being run over when crossing desert roads. When tourists visit deserts, they often travel in off-road vehicles. These can crush plants and their delicate roots, making it harder for them to grow. Vehicles can also collapse underground burrows where animals, such as desert tortoises and toads, spend much of their time.

Off-road vehicles damage desert soils and sand, so they blow or wash away more easily. They are also noisy and can disturb shy desert animals, such as kangaroo rats.

DESERT FUTURES

Around the world, many people are working hard to protect fragile desert biomes. They are striving to ensure the survival of the living things that have adapted to these inhospitable environments.

These scientists are studying the **endangered** African spurred tortoise in the Sahel Desert, West Africa.

Scientific study

Scientists study desert biomes to find out what the problems are and what causes them. For example, they measure animals, such as desert tortoises, to see if changes in a desert affect their growth. They fit animals with radio collars that can track their movements to see how far they have to go to find food.

Solar Power

Some scientists are looking at ways to build huge **solar power** plants in deserts to make electricity using the uninterrupted sunlight. This would cut down the amount of oil and coal used to make electricity and reduce the impacts of global warming.

Brown hyenas are desert animals under threat, but many live safely in the Kgalagadi Transfrontier Park.

Conservation counts

Conservation groups work to conserve, or protect, wild places. Some work with governments to create **national parks**. These are areas of protected land where people cannot build, dig mines, or take too much water. Conservation groups also raise money to help protect endangered desert animals.

We can all help desert biomes by supporting conservation organizations. We can also help by reducing our use of fossil fuels to slow global warming. For example, we can carpool or walk to school rather than go by car. What can you do to help?

Fact File: Kgalagadi Transfrontier Park

Location: Botswana and South Africa
Size: 15,000 sq. mi. (38,000 km²)
Overview: A huge park with dry landscapes and red sand dunes in addition to animals, such as jackals, brown hyenas, and wild cats.

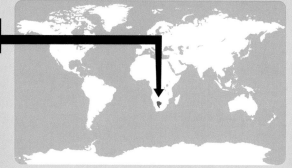

GLOSSARY

adaptation Special feature or way of behaving that helps a living thing survive in its habitat

aquifer An underground layer of rock or soil that has holes that store water

biome Large region of Earth with living things adapted to the typical climate, soils, and other features

blood vessels Tubes inside an animal that carry blood around its body

blubber Thick layer of fat under the skin

camouflage Color, pattern, or shape that makes it hard to identify an object against the background it is in

climate Typical weather pattern through the year in an area

condense To change from a gas into a liquid

conservation The act of guarding, protecting, or preserving something

continent One of the seven large masses of land on the planet: Asia, Africa, North America, South America, Europe, Australia and Antarctica

drought When an area gets so little water or rain that plants die

dune Hills formed from sand

endangered At risk of dying out

energy The power to grow, move, and do things

equator An imaginary line around the center of Earth

evaporate Turn from a liquid into a gas

food chain A way of showing the movement of the sun's energy from one living thing to another

food web A network of related food chains that show how energy is passed from one living thing to another.

global warming Rise in average temperature of Earth caused by human use of machines and electricity, which is altering weather patterns worldwide

habitat Place where an animal or plant lives

hibernate To go into a special type of deep sleep when body processes in an animal slow down to reduce use of stored food over winter

insect Animal such as a fly or beetle that has six legs and usually one or two pairs of wings

insulate To prevent the movement of heat

lichen Life-form that is a partnership between two or more types of living things, such as fungi and algae

mammal Group of animals that have hair or fur and feed their babies with milk from their bodies

mineral A substance such as salt that is non-living and forms naturally usually obtained from the ground

national park An area in nature where the wildlife is protected by law

nectar Sugary substance found in the center of flowers

nomad People who move from place to place

oasis Area in a desert where there is water and plants

pits Dips or indentations

pollute To allow substances, such as oil or smoke, to damage water, soil, or the air.

predator Animal that catches and eats other animals

prey An animal eaten by another animal

reflect Bounce off

reptile A cold-blooded animal that lays eggs, and has a body covered with scales or bony plates

resources Things that people use or need, such as water and food

solar power Electricity made from sunlight

South Pole Southernmost point of Earth

succulent Plant with thick fleshy leaves or stems adapted to storing water

venom Poison made by some animals for defence or to stun or kill prey

water vapor A gas in the air, formed when liquid water evaporates

FIND OUT MORE

Books

Deserts Inside Out (Ecosystems Inside Out)
Marina Cohen
Crabtree Publishing , 2015

Deserts Around the World Series
Crabtree Publishing , 2012

Desert Climates (Heinemann Infosearch: Focus on Climate Zones)
Anita Ganeri
Scholastic, 2016

Websites

Read more about deserts at:
kids.nceas.ucsb.edu/biomes/desert.html

There is more information about deserts at:
www.cotf.edu/ete/modules/msese/earthsysflr/desert.html

Find out more about desert habitats at:
**www.kids.nationalgeographic.com/explore/nature/habitats/
desert/#deserts-camel-sahara.jpg**

Discover more about deserts and watch a fun video at:
www.easyscienceforkids.com/all-about-deserts/

INDEX